Into the
Uncut Grass

Trevor Noah

Into the Uncut Grass

illustrated by Sabina Hahn

JOHN MURRAY

First published in Great Britain in 2024 by John Murray (Publishers)

1

Copyright © Trevor Noah 2024
Illustration © Sabina Hahn 2024

A CIP catalogue record for this title is available from the British Library

Hardback ISBN 9781399821339
ebook ISBN 9781399821353

Book design by Simon M. Sullivan

Printed and bound in Italy by L.E.G.O Spa

John Murray policy is to use papers that are natural, renewable and recyclable products and made from wood grown in sustainable forests. The logging and manufacturing processes are expected to conform to the environmental regulations of the country of origin.

Carmelite House
50 Victoria Embankment
London EC4Y 0DZ

www.johnmurraypress.co.uk

John Murray Press, part of Hodder & Stoughton Limited
An Hachette UK company

The authorised representative in the EEA is Hachette Ireland,
8 Castlecourt Centre, Castleknock Road, Castleknock,
Dublin 15, D15 YF6A, Ireland

This is dedicated to the imagination
that lives in all of us.

Introduction

This book was inspired by a conflict. Specifically, the never-ending war between me and my mother. When I was young, my mother and I used to spend a lot of time in a state of debate. As much as I wanted to respect her wishes, I always had my own plans in my tiny little head. Her wishes and my plans were rarely the same.

She would tell me to tie my shoelaces, I would argue that the knots made it harder to get my shoes off. She would demand that I clean my room, I would insist that it looked better in chaos. My mother would ask me to mow the lawn and I'd reply with a comprehensive list of all the reasons the grass looked better tall and uncut. Round and round we'd go, in a funny dance: She'd throw out a rule, I'd find a loophole and jump through it. But when all the loopholes were closed and justice was closing in, I would switch tactics: Instead of arguing, I'd find the closest open door and *run*. My grandmother called me "Springbok" for a reason.

Here's a picture of a springbok. It may be the only picture you'll ever see of a springbok standing still.

There was something so tantalizing about that world outside my house, the wild unknown that started just a few feet from our front door. All my life I'd run out into it, scared and thrilled at what I'd find. And all my life I would realize that I was running in a circle. From my first eager step over the threshold and into the street, I was on a journey that would take me back home again: different, maybe wiser, but mostly just happy to be under my own roof again with the people I loved the most. Conflict and disagreement, I learned, are necessary parts of life—but what matters isn't whether we disagree but rather how we handle that disagreement. Conflict drove me to debate and then discovery and then back to love.

But there is more than one way to discover the world.

This book was also born in the quieter moments of my childhood, the ones in which my body was still but my mind and imagination were in beautiful motion.

Every time someone asks me about my favorite memories as a kid, I have to think hard and long to separate out my real memories from my imagined ones. Because decades before I first stepped onto an airplane or a ship as an adult, I had already traveled the world. I had climbed the highest mountains in the Himalayas and dived to the deepest depths of the sea. I had flown on the backs of griffins into battle and escaped giants who wanted revenge for my stealing their bread.

Imagining has always been one of my greatest joys. It's the one thing we all can do, no matter where we're from or who we are. It allows us to explore worlds we've never seen and live as people we've never been.

Imagining, I've come to understand, is crucial for conflict resolution. When faced with seemingly insurmountable challenges, it is our ability to envision possibilities beyond the immediate and the obvious that paves the way for solutions. Imagination allows us to step outside of entrenched positions and explore new perspectives, to conceive of compromises that were previously invisible. In those moments of heated debate or silent tension, it is the imaginative mind that can visualize a reality where both sides find common ground, a landscape of understanding and harmony that has never yet existed. By daring to dream of what could be rather than resigning ourselves to what is, we unlock the potential for true and lasting resolution by bridging divides and forging new paths where none seemed possible.

This is where books come in. If imagination is the rocket, then books are the rocket fuel. They supercharge the mind and help it see beyond what it can conceive on its own.

Before I could read for myself, my mother would read to me. Then, when I learned how to read, I would read to her. Together we would share the silliest stories—and sometimes serious ones too. We would discuss the characters we had encountered and the wonderful worlds we had explored. In my childhood world, defined by difference, these books were where my mother and I could meet without judgment, just two explorers sharing stories.

———

This is a book about that undiscovered country just beyond the shadow of home, and the lessons we learn in that unpredictable landscape. It's about disagreements and difference—but it's also about how we bridge those gaps and find what matters most, whether we're parents or kids, neighbors, gnomes, or political adversaries. It's a picture book, but it's not a children's book. Rather, it is a book for kids to share with parents and for parents to share with kids. A world for both to explore as their imaginations take them away. And if you're both a parent and a child, or maybe neither, you can still read it for yourself or to a stranger or to someone you love or to a passing snail—and hopefully be reminded of the crowded journey into the uncut grass that we're all on together.

—Trevor

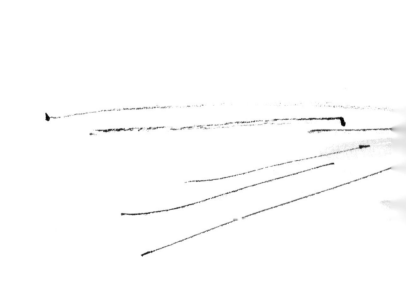

Into the Uncut Grass

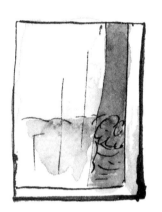

Part I

—

Awake

"Wake up, Walter," the boy said, his voice quivering with excitement. "It's time to start the day."

Walter, the old bear, loved dreaming beneath the warm blankets of the boy's bed. What Walter did not love was being rushed out of sleep, especially when he was dreaming, as one does, about waffles. Slowly he opened his eyes.

"The day should start when I wake up," Walter said through a yawn. "I should not have to wake up to start the day."

"Save your riddles for later," the boy said, his eyes dancing. "We've got to get outside. You do know what today is, don't you?"

"Well, clearly it's not the day I get to finish my dream," the bear said, turning back to his pillow for a last sweet second of sleep.

"You're right," the boy said. "It's even better than that. Today's the day we get to make our dreams come true."

Walter tried to close his eyes even tighter.

"It's SATURDAY!" the boy shouted.

In one fell swoop he flipped Walter out of the blankets, whipped open the curtains, and flung open the bedroom window so that he could project his voice into the world outside, like a king issuing decrees to his loyal subjects.

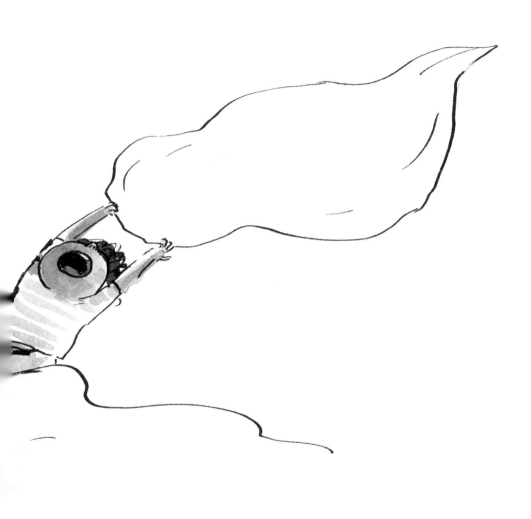

"Today we will climb to the very top of the tall, tall tree and finally catch a cloud. Then we must finish digging our hole to the middle of the earth to see if the giant gumball is real," he proclaimed.

"And this day," the boy continued, gesturing boldly to the empty yard outside his window, "this is the day we will finally defeat the leaf monster! So let's GOOOOO . . . !"

Walter tumbled from the bed and landed softly on his feet. He rubbed his eyes a bit sadly. The boy had forgotten something, and it was the old bear's job to remind him of the things he'd rather forget.

"Before we can go outside," Walter said, "we need to finish inside. You know the rules as well as I do."

Walter cleared his throat.

"Brush our teeth so our breath smells clean, wash our face in case we are seen, comb our hair to keep the lice away, and make our bed so we can start the day." His eyes softened as he watched the boy's face slide into a frown. "I don't know how you keep forgetting it, your mother even made it rhyme."

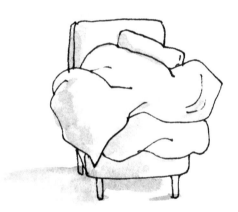

The boy was not amused. To him, this wasn't a cute poem for remembering, it was the tyrannical edict of an iron-fisted emperor.

"Not this again," he grumbled. "Every day I have to do exactly what my mother says even if I don't want to. Who says she knows best?"

"Well," the bear said, "she's gotten us this far."

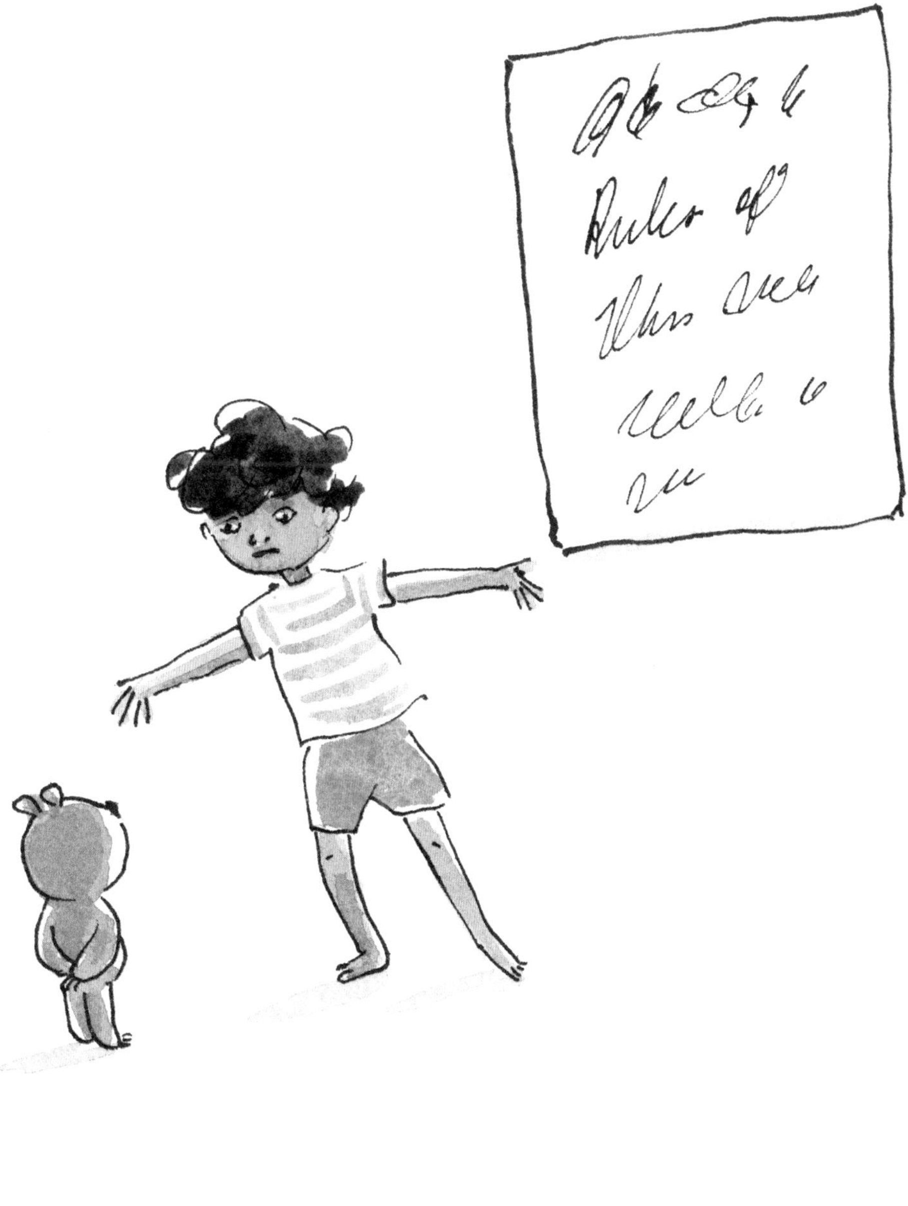

The boy was not convinced. "And what does she know about being a kid?"

"Actually, I think all grown-ups start as children, that's what they're grown up from," Walter replied.

"I don't know about that. I've known my mom my whole life and she's always been a grown-up!"

Before the bear could fully process that, the boy continued: "And it just makes no sense. Saturdays aren't for chores, they're for adventure. That's why there's no school on Saturdays, even the teachers understand that."

The boy's head was now buzzing with a different kind of energy. He leapt onto the unmade bed.

"Why should I brush my teeth? I just did it last night. And I don't care to wash my face, I'm not going to look at it. My hair is already on my head, so it's where it's supposed to be. And most of all," the boy said, jumping back to the floor, "I don't want to make my bed. And the bed doesn't want to be made. That's why it keeps unmaking itself. It wants to breathe! It wants to be free! Just like us!"

"Yes," replied the bear, "and we *can* be free, we just have to follow the rules of the house."

"Or," the boy said, "we can just leave this house of rules. Walter, new plan: Today we will run away!"

Before Walter could respond, the boy grabbed the old bear and made a mad dash out of the bedroom, running through the house like a gust of wind, as fast as his little legs would carry him, down the stairs, through the kitchen, and over the threshold of the door that led to the backyard.

He kept on running through the yard, his little feet barely touching the ground as he strained with all his might to escape the chores that threatened to ruin his perfect day.

Finally he stopped to catch his breath. He carefully lowered the old bear back onto its feet.

"I won't let it happen, Walter," the boy said. "I won't let rules spoil our perfect day."

Walter knew that he needed to remind the boy of something. "We can't just run away," he explained. "Your mother will miss you. And where will we sleep? And who will make us waffles?"

"We'll build our own house," the boy said. "And we'll grow our own waffles!"

"I don't think that's how you get waffles."

"And our beds will breathe the same air we do. The air of freedom!"

"But sooner or later your mother will find us," Walter said, looking back at the house. "She always does."

The boy's eyes lit up again. He had an idea.

"Then this time we need to go where we've never gone before," he said. "Into the uncut grass!"

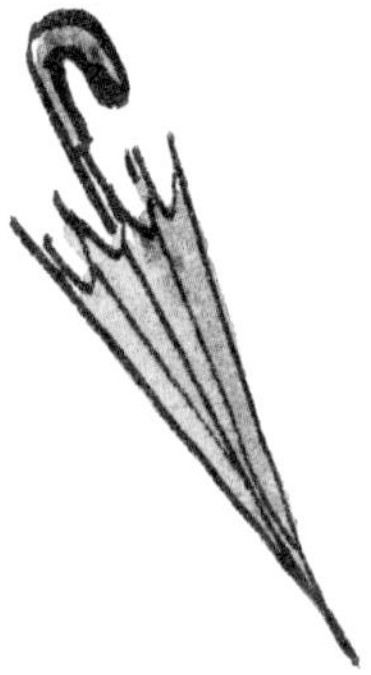

Part II

—

The Gate

The two friends held hands as they walked farther and farther away from the house. They passed the lawn chairs where the boy and his mother would sometimes read together, and the fire pit where they'd toast marshmallows. They passed the tire swing hanging from the short, thick-limbed tree. They even wandered past the old shed with the heavy lock on it.

Finally, they arrived.

The boy stopped and took it all in, his eyes widening like an adventurer who had just reached an ancient treasure.

"The rusty gate," the boy said. "We've never come this far alone."

"I think there was a reason for that," the bear said with a slight shudder.

The boy studied the gate. It seemed different today, its twisted metal and rusted edges vibrating with whispers of magic. They had never come this far alone, it's true, but the boy had been here before with his mother. He remembered holding her hand as she inspected the neat green rows of herbs and blossoming flowers in their garden. On those days his eyes would sometimes wander to the other side of the gate, to the wild, free, uncut grass that led into the shadowy woods. He'd walk closer to the gate and squint his eyes, trying to see into the grass and the shadows. *Wait, is that a creature over there?* he would wonder. *Are those gold coins catching the light? Is that a . . . ghost?* But then his mother would call him away from the gate, back to the safety of the garden.

Now the boy's eyes wandered in the opposite direction, away from the gate and back toward the house. He knew by now that the kitchen was filling with the smell of freshly made waffles. His mother's soft humming would be gently drifting from room to room. The colors in every part of the house would be gradually coming alive as the sun rose higher.

Home.

The bear watched as the boy quietly stared at the house.

"I don't think it's too late," Walter said. "We could turn back. . . ."

The boy took a breath. He decided to be brave. Or foolish.

"We've come too far, Walter. We're on our own now."

The boy willed himself toward the rusty gate and slowly grabbed hold of its bars. In that moment the only force stronger than the boy's fear was his determination. He held on tight, leaned his body backward, and pulled as hard as he could. Walter pulled on the gate along with his friend, even though his old bear muscles were not as strong as they once were. Particularly, he thought, without a good breakfast.

They pulled and pulled and . . . nothing.

Frustrated, the boy stomped his feet and shouted out, "Why won't this stubborn gate open?"

Maybe you're the stubborn one. The gate is just a gate.

For a moment the boy and the bear thought that the gate had spoken. Then they looked up.

At the top of the gate, a garden gnome had appeared. It hadn't made a sound until just then.

"Greetings, strange travelers," the gnome said. "What brings you to the uncut grass?"

"Hello!" the boy said loudly. He wondered if pulling on the gnarly old gate had summoned this mysterious creature, but he didn't have time to figure that out. Wherever it had come from, the gnome was here now and waiting for his answer. "We left home to find adventure, build a new life, and finally be free," the boy explained.

"Oh dear," the gnome said. "Were you in prison?"

"No . . . but yes!" the boy said. "A prison of rules! If I don't do exactly what my mother tells me to, I am forbidden to leave the house."

"Oh, that sounds hard," the gnome said, stroking his beard. "And what terrible things does your mother want you to do?"

"She wants us to make the bed," Walter said.

"Ah, making the bed," the gnome said with a gentle laugh. "I've heard that humans struggle with this sometimes. But why do you hate it so much?"

"Have you ever made a bed?" the boy asked.

"Well, on our side of the gate, no one even has a bed," the gnome replied. "We sleep in trees or caves or just lay our heads down in the tall grass."

"That sounds like a dream," the boy said. "Because making the bed is the worst part of every day. And the bed doesn't want to be made, either. It stretches itself and becomes bigger so the sheet doesn't fit. It swallows me with blankets whenever I try to cover it. And the whole time, the pillows frown like unhappy uncles."

"That sounds like a real struggle," the gnome said.

"It is!" the boy said. "And if every day begins with a battle, how can I ever find peace?"

The gnome looked at the boy with pity.

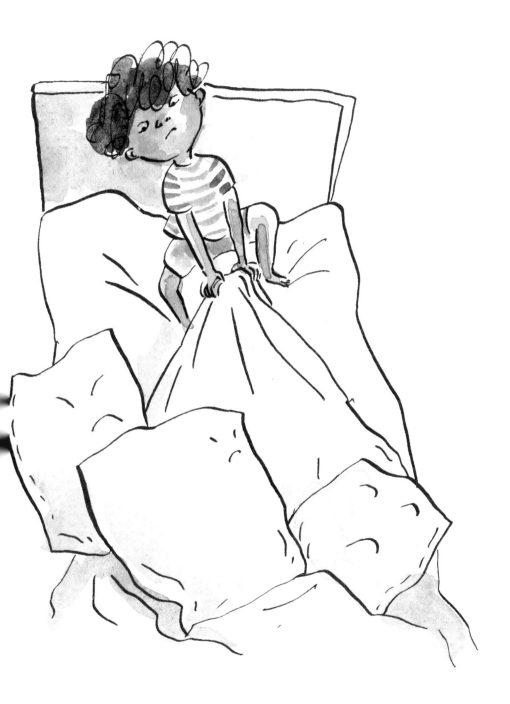

But then, just for a moment, Walter thought he might have seen a small smile peeking through the gnome's eyes before quickly disappearing.

The gnome spoke again. "What does your mother say when you tell her about your, um, terrible struggle?"

"We've never told her," Walter said.

"She wouldn't understand," the boy added. "She just wants to stop us from doing what we want."

"Oh," the gnome replied. "But why would she want to do that?"

The boy was baffled. "Why? Why do grown-ups do anything?"

"Good question," the gnome said. "Why don't you ask her?"

"What difference would it make?"

"It makes all the difference!" The gnome now lowered its voice, as if telling the boy an important secret. "Every person is just an obstacle unless you try to understand them. Even your own mother! It's like the way a gate can seem locked if you don't understand how it opens."

The boy stopped pulling on the gate and pushed instead. The gate easily swung open and he and Walter stumbled through, tumbling, finally, into the deep grass on the other side.

The gnome laughed. "Well, good luck on the rest of your journey. I hope you find the answers you seek. And good luck with that bed!"

The boy and the bear walked together for a moment in silence.

"Huh, that was interesting," the boy finally said.

"Yes, I know," the bear said. "A talking gnome, wow."

"No, not that. I mean, yes, that was weird, but we're not home anymore, Walter. You should be prepared to see strange things."

Walter shrugged, and the two friends continued walking.

"I wonder if things would be different if our mother understood," the boy said.

"Or if you did," Walter answered.

The forest of the uncut grass now stood just before them. They gazed at it quietly until the silence was broken by a ferocious grumble from Walter's stomach.

Part III

—

Into the Woods

The boy and his old friend found a trail in the grass and began to follow it. The grass grew deeper and wilder around them with every step. They could sense the magic of the forest unfolding as they walked along— petals of golden flowers floating through the air, bushes the size of buses, and on the soft breeze they could hear the whispers of trees who'd never forgotten how to talk.

But now they heard other voices, distant but more distinct.

"Do you hear that, Walter?" the boy said. "We should go check it out."

"Hmm, strange voices in a magical forest," Walter said. "I think we should go the other way."

But the boy held the bear's hand tighter and pressed on, following the sound of the voices down the trail and around a tall apple tree where they saw two snails with large colorful shells. One's shell was striped in brilliant red. The other's was marked by a bright pink spiral. The two snails were in the middle of a great debate.

"I say we go left!" said Stripe.

"And I say we go right!" said Spiral.

"My friend, I've gone left before," Stripe said, "and the grass makes the journey smoother."

"Well, my love, I've gone right before," Spiral said. "There's dirt and rocks and roots, but the path is shorter."

"OK, then I'll go right," Stripe said.

"And I'll go left," said Spiral.

"See you on the other side!" they said together.

"Excuse me," the boy asked, walking closer, "but what are you doing?"

"We're trying to get to the apple that fell from that tree," Stripe said, gesturing with its left tentacle. The boy followed the pointing tentacle with his eyes to the largest apple he'd ever seen.

"Turns out," Spiral said, "it fell a lot farther away than people say."

"I'm so confused," the boy said. "If *you* chose left and *you* chose right, why did you both end up going the opposite way?"

"Oh, that's simple," Stripe said. "When we can't agree, we don't argue forever, she just does it my way."

"And she does it mine," Spiral said.

"But if you both think you're right," the boy asked, "why bother doing it the other way?"

"Because everyone thinks they're right—" Spiral said.

"—until they discover they're wrong," Stripe said.

"Now if you'll excuse us," they said together, "we've got an apple to get to."

The boy and the bear climbed up to the tree's lowest branch and sat together to watch the race. The boy was mesmerized by the snails and their beautiful shells.

"Imagine living with your own home on your back," the boy told his bear. "A house just for you, with no one else's rules to follow."

"But then you could never have a sleepover," Walter reminded him. Then, more quietly, he added, "Or a place to go home to after an adventure."

The two friends returned their attention to the race about to begin below them. From their branch they could see both snails stretching their strange little muscles as they prepared to start their journeys.

Stripe took off. She clambered and climbed over rocks and roots, dodging wormholes and sharp twigs. The road was rough, but she found a rhythm and moved quickly. Well, quickly for a snail. Which is pretty slow.

Spiral slid carefully through a smooth section of uncut grass. She stopped once to smell a flower and once to lick a drop of dew from a leaf. Then she stopped again to watch a cluster of butterflies twirling overhead. When she arrived at the apple, Stripe was already there waiting.

"You were right," Stripe said, shaking pebbles from her tentacles and dirt from her shell. "The dirt path is so much shorter. Let's use it next time."

"But you were right too," Spiral said, her eyes still wide with delight. "The grass path was beautiful and smooth. I saw butterflies! Flowers! So much sky!"

The snails began devouring the apple together, stopping every now and then to share stories of their different adventures. The boy and Walter listened for a while, because the snails, who had traveled many roads in their lives—sometimes together, sometimes apart, but always very, very slowly—were excellent storytellers. But now it was time to keep walking.

"Walter . . ."

"Yes, friend."

"What do you think we would have seen if we tried things Mom's way?"

They walked a little farther, their feet sometimes tangling in the growing grass, pondering other paths they could have taken. The boy remembered his abandoned list of adventures. Walter thought about waffles.

Then the boy heard a growl.

"Walter, you really need to control your stomach."

"Um, that wasn't me," Walter said.

"Aaahhh!"

"Did we win?" the boy asked.
"Yes," the bear answered.

Part IV

—

Crossroads

"Look, there are two paths," the boy said.

"Which should we take?" Walter asked.

"I think this one will take us deeper into the uncut grass," the boy said uncertainly.

"And this one will take us back home," Walter said hopefully.

"I don't know," the boy said. "We've come so far already. Maybe we just have to keep going."

Walter studied the boy's face for a moment, then asked, "But do you want to keep going?"

"I . . . I don't remember," the boy said. He began pacing in the deep grass to gather his thoughts, which were now scattering across his mind.

"Hey, watch out!"

The boy and the bear heard a tiny, tinny voice coming from somewhere beneath them. They got down on their knees and pushed the long grass to the side to see the source of the sound.

"Heads or tails? Heads or tails? Flip the coin, it never fails," chanted a collection of coins gathered in the grass.

The coins, of different metals and sizes, were arranged in a circle surrounding one larger old coin who smiled as the others shouted. Suddenly the coins reached forward and, with one heave, lifted the large coin and flipped it into the air! When it landed, they all cheered.

"It's decided! We will dance!" they shouted. Then they threw themselves against one another, making a delightful jingling sound.

"Hey there," the large old coin said to the boy, dusting himself off. "I know you from a long time ago. Only you used to be bigger and much more hairy."

"I don't think I've ever been hairy," the boy said, "and this is the biggest I've ever been."

"Yes, I'm sure it's you and you've shrunk. Remember I used to live in your pocket?"

"Oh, wait, you must be thinking of my grandfather," the boy said. "He's definitely hairy."

"Ah, of course, that makes much more sense," the coin said. "Well, it's nice to meet you, grandson of Hairy."

"Nice to meet you too. Is this a party?" the boy asked.

"We are celebrating our latest decision," the old coin said. "Half of the coins wanted to have ice cream and watch the sun set over the grass. The other half of the coins wanted to have pie and a dance party."

"How did you decide?" the boy asked.

"The way we make all of our decisions," the old coin said. "We flip, well, . . . me! That's our rule: Heads or tails, fate decides. And how it lands we all abide."

"That sounds fun," the boy said. "But does anyone get mad when they don't get their way?"

A smaller coin rolled over and spoke up. "You can't get mad at luck!"

"We have traveled from one pocket to another all over the world," said the older coin, "and everywhere we've been, we've seen people arguing over silly things."

"One person wants to ride the bus, the other wants to take the train," the smaller coin said. "One person wants to buy candy, the other person wants to buy a potato."

"Friends argue with each other," the old coin continued. "Parents argue with kids. Dogs argue with cats. And for what?"

"So we decided we'd rather compromise together than get what we want all alone," the smaller coin said. "After all, we're coins! We need one another to add up to anything at all!"

"But what if you follow the coin flip and things go wrong?" the boy asked.

"Well, that's the beauty of life," the old coin said. "Sometimes you make the right choice and things go wrong, and sometimes you make the wrong choice and things go right."

"There are two sides to every coin," Walter said.

"And the third side," the smaller coin said. "The edges. . . . Everyone forgets the edges."

"Or maybe there's just one side," the old coin said. "We can't always decide what will happen in life. But we can always decide who it will happen with."

The boy looked back at the crossroads. One path led deeper into the uncut grass. One path led back to the house, the unmade bed, Walter's waffles, and their mother. He turned to the older coin.

"Do you think . . . I could try it?"

"Of course," the old coin said. "Flip away!"

The boy thought it might be rude to throw the old coin into the air, so he flipped himself instead. He tumbled from head to foot and back again while all the coins chanted. Even Walter joined in.

"Heads or tails? Heads or tails? It's the way that never fails."

Finally the boy landed in the dirt and laughed while the coins all cheered.

"Walter," he said, "I think I know what we should do now."

The boy looked back at the crossroads.

"Do you think it's too late to go home?"

And one more time, Walter reminded the boy of what he already knew. "If you still call it home," he said, "you can always go back."

© MARY ELLEN MATTHEWS

Trevor Noah is a comedian from South Africa and the author of the international bestseller *Born a Crime*.

SABINA HAHN grew up in Riga, Latvia, and now lives in New York. Ever since she was a child, she has been a voracious reader and an unstoppable doodler, which has led her into the world of children's books. Her greatest talent lies in conveying the understated humor and tenderness of both daily life and realms of fantasy.